SATAN'S SWEETHEARTS

POEMS BY

MARGE SIMON & MARY TURZILLO

Satan's Sweethearts
Marge Simon & Mary Turzillo

ISBN-13: 978-0-9983373-8-8

Printed in the U.S.A.

Weasel Press
Manvel, TX
www.weaselpress.com

Table of Contents

A Mother Only Satan Could Love

The Ones Who Kill Their Own 13
Bloody Mama 14
Mother Marti 16
Flower Gardens 17
Paper Doll 18
Flower Boxes 20
Never Choke A Stranger 21
The Piano Teacher 22
Half-Hangit Maggie 24
Velma Immortalized 26

Sisters of Dreadful Mercy

Broth and an Occasional Teaspoon of Orange Juice 29
Fifty Nine Days in the Children's Ward 32
With God and Texas On My Side 33
Not-So-Sweet Jane 34
The Joys of Arsenic 36
Amelia Dyer, Baby Farmer (1837 – 1896) 37
Trick or Treat 40
Jimmy's Angels 42

Sister Dread and Daughter Death

Lizzie's New Toy 47
Mary's Tale 48
Sister, Mine 50
Three Sisters, a Kingdom, and a Glass of Wine 51
The Sister 53
Jeanette in Trousers, Howling 55

The Last Wife's Club

"M" is for Murderess 61
The Hero's Head 62
Agrippina Chats with a Portrait of the Former Empress 63
Gesche's Deathmask 65
Mad Love 67
Katherine Knight's Demon 69
Zinc caskets in the basement. 71
How to Bake a Wedding Cake 73
The Marriage of Suicide Sal 74
Queen of Clubs 76
Winnie and the Big Black Trunk 78
June Wedding, far from the Temple 80

Dames from the Deepest Circle of Hell

Delphine Lalaurie's Upstairs Room 83
Red Witch of Buchenwald 84
Lady Bathory's Procurer 85
"The Most Evil Woman in Britain" 86
Dragon in Phoenix Skin 87
Lady M 89
Five days of Forever Love 90
Breathless 91
Cathy Wood: Still Breathing 94
Mary Farmer Took An Axe 95
Born Mean 97
Kindred Spirits 99
Caril Fugate's Angel 101
A Legend in My Time 102
Coveted Cianciulli Recipes 104
Memories 105
Little Sandra Cantu 106
Remembering Lady Jane Grey, as We Lay Dying 107
Rebirth 108
Empty Pistol 109
The Choice 111
The Woman's Fault 113

Dedication

We respectfully wish to dedicate this collection to Mary's sister, Jane Ann Turzillo, who inspired the idea for this book and several of the evil women that she has written about or found, and to the families of the victims of these most heinous crimes.

— MS & MT

INTRODUCTION

Marge says: I believe it stands to reason that monstrous women — like monstrous men, have been around since before recorded time. So when Mary approached me with the idea of writing poems based on Evil Women in history, I was instantly ready for another collaborative poetry collection.

Once we got into it, we realized that we had taken on a very difficult project. Women of any race or era can be very creatively nasty and despicable. Some were so bad that we had to step away and do something else before returning to finish the poem. *I am quite serious about that.* Read my poem about Delphine LaLaurie and what she kept upstairs in her New Orleans mansion!

We include women like the serial killers Gwendolyn Graham and Cathy Wood in our other collaborations. Whether it's because something terrible was once done to them or because they just needed to feel more powerful, they made victims of the helpless elderly who were entrusted to a healthcare facility. Thus their damage was more profound than whatever they did to their victims. In a real way, society itself becomes their ultimate victim. You will find other women like Graham and Wood in these poems:

"Bloody Mama"
"Linda Burfield Hazzard"
"Louise Masset"
"Mary Farmer"

I'm afraid there is nothing light-hearted about any of our poems in this collection. Is it a fault of society, of what life you're born into? Is it genetic –a few rogue chromosomes? That conundrum bothers me. Maybe you will be bothered too.

Mary says: Crime fiction and fiction in general, has a convention that when murder or mayhem occurs, the victim is typically female and the perpetrator typically male. I know this isn't universal, but readers come to expect a tale of an innocent weak woman falling to a conniving evil man. In society in general, when domestic disturbances occur, the expectation is that the man incited it and is the final offender. Yet these stereotypes do not fit reality. Women do murder. Domestic violence may be the fault of both parties, and it's often the women who picks up the gun or the frying pan of hot grease, in self-defense, she may claim, but how are we to know? Murderpedia lists almost half as many women as men as murderers. When women become tyrants (read: political leaders) they often commit atrocities as horrific as the scope of their powers (a trend I tell of in poems of Queen Ranavalona and Bloody Mary, not to speak of the various pirate and criminal queens that we so gleefully celebrate, as if a man pirate is evil, but a woman pirate is to be admired for her "spunk."

According to one source (**"Homicide Trends in the United States, 1980-2008" United States Department of Justice** (2010), about 90% of homicides are committed by men. Yet, in murders of children under 5 by biological parents, almost half of perpetrators are women (ibid.). This suggests that women murder almost as frequently as men when their victim is more helpless than they are. One also wonders if the low conviction rate for women murderers might be due to their superior cleverness at concealing their guilt, as poisons, for example, are a favored weapon of women.

I've been the victim of spousal abuse, so I'm not speaking out of school. But I've also seen men abused by their wives and girlfriends. Not weaklings, not handicapped men, but big strong men who could or would not even lift a hand to defend themselves. Call it chivalry; what choice did these man have? If they had struck back, they would have been the offenders. And I've seen false accusations, on the advice of dishonorable attorneys, used to discredit a husband and take away his property or access to his children.

We live in a world of stereotypes. Jodi Arias claimed to be a victim of domestic abuse, and yet her defense was 19 stab wounds and a bullet to her beloved's head.

Marge and I decided to explore this very dark aspect of human life. It wasn't easy. There were times when I was so horrified and depressed by what my gender was capable of that I dodged the project. Thus it was when I read Marge's poem "Delphine Lalaurie's Upstairs Room." Marge has several times written poems that sent me reeling, but she also kept me on task, and I'm glad she did. I hope these poems, which are not about facts, but rather the feelings we have about evil women, will open some discussion and some thought in the readers' minds.

A final note: my heart goes out to the living relatives of these women. I can't imagine the pain that the husband, parents, and children of these offenders must deal with every day. Perhaps they believe her to be innocent, but no matter: they must live with what the public thinks of their near relation.

These are dark poems, but I hope they speak to you, reader, whether you are a man or a woman.

A MOTHER ONLY SATAN COULD LOVE

The Ones Who Kill Their Own

When I was a little girl, my parents got a Siamese cat. They wanted to breed her. So when the time came, that was done. By and by, she had a litter of six kittens. But as we watched each born, she would not clean them. She did nothing. So we did that, and put the tiny ones back into the birthing box with clean towels.

Come the morning, she was cleaning herself. Six small bodies lay mutilated, dead. There was blood on her tongue.

-Marge Simon

Ma Barker (1873-1935)

Bloody Mama

Killed in a shoot-out
a Tommy gun beside you,
such a ruthless matriarch,
ended by a single shot.

Ruthless matriarch, me?
I gave them birth, not moral sense.
Their deeds made headline news,
but I just rocked the cradle, not the world.

"A vicious mastermind
of crime," so said J. Edgar,
commander of the F.B.I,
an authority to heed.

You, J. Edgar, call me a mastermind?
You, who think that women shouldn't vote?
Thank Jesus I'm no Negro babe,
and no card-carrying hotsie leftist Red!

Herman, Lloyd, Art and Fred
before and after robberies,
kept you sumptuously pleased,
wanting their dinner hot
when they got home.

Am I to blame for loving my dear boys?
Sure, they wrought havoc when they could.
You swore to hunt them down, you pig.
With Bureau agents armed with Tommy guns.

You so loved the lifestyle,
the fruit of your boys' crimes,
had many a lover along the way,
some approved of, some not;
apparently you felt you deserved
some wanton fun.

Some wanton fun, you vicious dick!
I saw Feds slaughter Fred, my precious son,
before they send a bullet to my heart.

I loved my sons just as you love your Clyde.
Family? you had no love except for him,
and now I lie here, cold as your black heart,
on Timberhill, in Oklahoma dirt.

So what? You'd have had no legend otherwise,
would have died in the lonesome Ozarks of your birth
a victim of poverty, no docudramas of your fame
to celebrate your misappropriated life.

-Marge Simon & Mary Turzillo

Enriqueta Marti 1868-1913

Mother Marti

They were my children by right of possession,
and soon forgot their parents, I made sure of that.
Some I beat, some I only pinched for discipline.
While in my care, their lives were fine.

I dressed the handsome ones in grand attire,
be they boy or girl of less than eight years old,
and for a price, the rich could take their pleasure
in my Mezzanine on Ponent Street.

Those too old or homely for the fornication game,
or those that caused my personal disfavor,
I disposed of with good intention, making remedies
from their blood and bones to cure the ills
of wealthy Barcelona gentry.

They were my children, my charges, and I fed them –
potatoes and stale bread, but sustenance enough,
those ones I deemed desirable, or useful otherwise.

Why do my cellmates stare at me that way?
Why do they hold those clubs, that rope?
Are we not all sisters under this wretched roof?

-Marge Simon

Mary Ann Cotton 1832-1893

Flower Gardens

Ms. Mary contrary
had one at a time.
Her garden of children
grew to twelve.

"Stomach fevers"
claimed all of her little ones,
along her path of woe.

Arsenic in her watering can,
left nothing for her to garden
but a bed of tangled thorns.

-Marge Simon

Mary Ann Cotton (1832-1873)

Paper Doll

The green wallpaper, she said, did Freddy in.
Flakes of it fell into his great snoring mouth.

Her element was paper:
wedding certificates,
birth notices,
the banknotes she spent too freely,
the promissory notes when pounds and pence ran out,
pawn tickets for her husbands' furniture,
the papers to insure her husbands' lives
for she had men aplenty,
more than her share of husbands,
four, though the last, poor Freddy Cotton,
was somewhat deceived, her third
not quite yet in the ground.

The children were a bother;
she couldn't get much life insurance
for most: they died with bellies full of agony.

Of Freddy's son, Charles Edward, she opined,
"He won't last long, like all the Cottons:
inflamed digestion." Then, when he died:
"Stomach fever," she told the coroner.

Turns out this lady's passe-partout was cheap fly-paper:
infused with arsenic
she harvested by soaking.

So, yes, it was the paper
that killed Fred Cotton, plus twenty others:

husbands, mother, friends, and children.
But not wallpaper.

Green wallpaper could tell many a tale if it could speak.
But fly-paper was Mary Ann's best friend:
shopkeepers must have thought her pestered with a lot of flies,
right up until the coroner exhumed Fred Cotton.
And made her infamous in paper tabloids
and for two centuries in books,
which, come to think,
are made of paper, like her deadly means.

-Mary Turzillo

Megan Huntsman 1975 —

Flower Boxes

They died
before blooming,
for I crushed their stems;
each cried only once,
then into the baggie,
and into the box.

It wasn't the pot,
nor was it the meth,
they had to be virginal births —
of all my six born,
not a one lived
to open its eyes to the sun.

-Marge Simon

Kathleen Folbigg 1967 –

Never Choke A Stranger

I'm not a serial killer.
never killed a living soul,
not like crazy Katherine Knight,
r that nasty Yank, Aileen.

ly babies dead and buried,
ot Deaths, every one.
ur friends testified it so,
t later came to doubt.

e, there was my silly diary,
husband found it tucked away.
Those details only make-believe,
at least I'm pretty sure of that.

Caleb, Patrick, Sarah and Liz —
but none beyond a toddler's age.
Besides, I never choked a stranger
like real serial killers do.

-Marge Simon

Louise Masset 1866-1900

The Piano Teacher

Little Manfred's father wouldn't marry me.
I didn't mind, he wasn't much in bed,
—about the French gentry, that's often true—
but he sent me a stipend for our baby.

Her slender fingers danced upon the keys
Playing "Oh Promise Me," a foreign tune.

I paid dear Miss Gentle to keep my son,
for he was my folly and my charge.
I saw him on Wednesday when I was free,
and ever a loving mother appeared.

Her loving fingers prowled piano keys,
played "She May Have Seen Better Days."

Is it my fault for God-given needs,
a discrete encounter between the sheets,
especially after meeting Eudore,
I couldn't wait to jump his bones!

She played, with fingers yearning,
"Believe Me if All those Endearing Young Charms."

Yet my lover was still such a young man,
wanting no part of another man's child,
and my little boy was the problem.
This matter I faced and dealt with.

Her fingers twitched, long and full of song,
A D'Oyly Carte show tune: "With Cat-like Tread."

I set out to send Manfred to France
to visit his papa, a righteous lie,
then secluded in London Bridge Station,
took a brick to his head, my hands on his nose,
I put an end to the business, right there.

Musician's fingers strong as steel, entuning
"She's More to be Pitied than Censured."
Strong fingers, strong hands,
Solving her issues, then humming,
"A Hot Time in the Old Town Tonight."

Consider the names he'd be called!
"bastard" or "son of a whore"!
I spared my poor son such a fate.
My final words, "what I suffer is just –"
and it was all for a decent fuck.

-Marge Simon & Mary Turzillo

Margaret Dickson (1702-1724, then died again c. 1753)

Half-Hangit Maggie

You haunt me, Maggie Dickson,
who had commerce, willing or not, with that man/boy,
you, who dreaded the shaming to your neighbors,
who hid your growing belly under a thick apron,
who suffered labor pains in a trance,
claiming you knew nothing of the birth,
who lost all memory of time and the place,
you, whose child slipped so easily into the cold River Tweed.

Was it God's will, Maggie,
that the coroner found the babe's lungs filled with air
so it must have died before he went in the river?
Was it God's will,
that Edinburgh court and the jury found you wanton,
that the people hated your fornication
or perhaps hated your vulgar howls mongering fish,
God's will that they believed
you had strangled the fruit of your womb,
and deserved not just hell after death,
but the tight rough knot, half-strangulation, the neck-snapping drop?

Was it God's will, Maggie,
that Grassmarket gibbet was crowded that day,
that the hangman boggled his trade,
or that your neck was too stout,
or maybe too slender, for the noose,
God's will, or blind luck,
that you had friends to drive you to the boneyard,
that you lay insensible in your wood box til just the right time,
when the sounds of your fists on the lid
made them open the coffin?

And was it God's will, pretty Maggie
the law said you could be hanged only once
ou now were a dead woman,
to remarry the fisherman who had abandoned you?

ıs it right, jolly Maggie,
at the rest of your life you were called Half-Hangit Maggie,
ıd a pub still stands in Grassmarket
ith a brass plaque telling your your story?

Maggie, my Maggie, remember,
you flung away that poor infant.
He was yours, fruit of your womb,
no dead cat to be cast into in the river.
Grassmarket tour guides today
make you a joke (how's that wry neck, Maggie?) or a heroine:
"Have a drink at the Maggie Dickson Pub," they urge,
as they pocket my fistful of pound coins.
And I wonder, Maggie, if you turned your face away
when they called you Half-hangit Maggie,
not enjoying the joke.
And mostly, I wonder, my Maggie,
if the babe has a name
and if you haunted its grave
the rest of your life.

-Mary Turzillo

Velma Barfield 1932-1984

Velma Immortalized

"You married my granddaddy. Him I never knew.
About the time he met me was about the time he met you.

Then you killed Stuart Taylor. Someone had to know.
Every man you been with, one by one they go. "
- from "Velma", Jonathan Byrd, Wildflowers album, 2001

Velma escaped her father's beatings,
married well, or so most thought
until her husband took to drink;
he died in flames when she was out;
the house rebuilt burned once again,
insured, and Velma got it all.

A mystery how kith and kin
and some not close at all — fell ill
with serious mal a les stomach,
including husband Number Two,
and not a one lived past a day.

Discovered, tried and sentenced,
Velma left this world devout,
wearing pink pajamas and Depends,
her final meal, Cheese Doodles
and an ice cold Coca-Cola.

Barfield's grandson Jonathan
immortalized old Velma's deeds,
his song proclaims her legend
like the taste of her arsenic,
a plainly bitter homage.

-Marge Simon

SISTERS OF DREADFUL MERCY

Dr. Linda Burfield Hazzard (1867 -1938)

Broth and an Occasional Teaspoon of Orange Juice

Dr. Hazzard had a clinic
administering audacious,
forward-thinking cures.

Cancer? Obesity? Hair loss? Mini-penis? Mental fog?
All healed by Dr. Linda's miracle regime.

The cure? So simple: starve!
Live on veggie broth just twice a day.

hair loss will happen anyway and cancer,
why that's a natural thing as well,
you get it fat, you get it thin –
A man's endowment is enhanced by starvation,
genitals appear much larger than they were -
as for mental fog—no common sense?
that's why you're here.

If you lacked the moral strength to fast,
Dr. Linda ran this sanitorium.

She locked you up
she took your cash
she stowed your jewels
she censored mail outgoing.

She only asked
about your bank account and deeds.

That only happened to my sister.
She lost more weight than I,

though both of us were under sixty pounds,
she was the first to die, but at least she got the treatment
that she was hoping for,
being able to squeeze into her burial gown,
the same dress she wore as an infant,

And if you tried to run
(that's if you had the strength),
a bullet to the head became a final cure.

It wasn't very sanitary
yet it did complete the job
to stay on diet: there are nutrients to be found
in the soil of one's grave.

To prove her panacea worked,
in the bathtub
of Wilderness Heights
her miracle cure resort,
which some called just Starvation Heights,
she did her own autopsies.

And confirmed her own diagnoses
just before cremation.

The process?

First: dehydration:
glucose used up
after just six hours in Dr. Linda's sanatorium.
You use ketone bodies to run your brain.
And so, as self conserves its fats:
eventually: delirium.

(However, if you'd ever used your brain
you wouldn't be in Dr. Hazzard's sanitorium.)

Yet it was beautifully advertized
with impressive credentials

even if she didn't have a medical degree,

Then, once your fats are all used up,
it's time for autophagy.
Think what that means:
auto=self
phagy=eat.
Self-cannibalism!

You're eating your own body!
(From within.)

I preferred not to think of that
when I noticed my eyes turning yellow
and I started pissing blood.

Next, marasmus: loss of energy, then putrifaction.
Kwashiorkor: oh, sure, you've read the news.

So, until the Williamsons got wind of her
and tried to rescue sisters Claire and Dorothea,
Dr. Linda's scheme worked like a charm.

It did indeed, but only one of us was saved
by smuggling a telegram beyond the gates of hell.

From our detached and lofty vantage
it seems that Dr. Linda was a quack,
or even worse, a predator.

But then, she chose to cure her own complaints
by the same anorexia she prescribed
to her unwary invalids:
and died a withered, bloated husk.

Justice for all who perished, if such a thing can be.

-Mary Turzillo & Marge Simon

Beverly Allitt (1968 –)

Fifty Nine Days in the Children's Ward

At Kesteven Hospital, Lincolnshire,
a young nurse stands in the gentle rain,
drops tickling her eyelashes as she gazes up
to the lights of the fourth floor.

Today had been a good one,
with two of her charges very ill
and another sure to die.

Tomorrow, back to work
to guide the little ones,
sending them to dreamland
or suspending them in nightmare
with insulin overdoses,
at first so easily concealed.

How could she be blamed?
Her victims' parents grateful
for her loving words and tender care.
Some claimed she was ill –
showing symptoms of mental disorder,
Münchausen syndrome full blown.
seeking recognition
or just the favor of a hug.

At Rampton Secure Hospital, Nottinghamshire
a former nurse sits confined to the fourth floor.
She goes to the window, watches the rain falling
but there is steel webbing on the pane,
reflecting her untroubled face.

-Marge Simon

Genene Ann Jones 1950 –

With God and Texas On My Side

My own idea, that "child care unit",
reason enough to use certain drugs
to treat the little ones; when some died,
I knew I'd got the dosage right.

Sure, I stuck the poison in their little butts,
just doing my job, the professional LVN,
but when the hospital noticed so many dying,
they asked us kiddie nurses to resign
for fear of being sued.

A pediatric clinic hired me,
no questions asked, and so
I continued my desire to "cure"—
only a few distinctive deaths,
but this time I was caught.

Stuck in a Texas prison
for ninety years and more,
but prisons here are overflowing
with drug dealers and addicts,
and thanks to a new law, I'll soon be free,
time enough to get back into my old routine,
keeping body and mind active at my age,
wouldn't you say?

-Marge Simon

Jane Toppan 1857-1938

Not-So-Sweet Jane

Her father was a mental case,
so they said; a widower and drunk,
he gave his little daughters
to the care of an orphanage.

One became a servant
took on the family's name,
was known as Jane Toppan.

Training to be a nurse at Cambridge,
she slit a frog and watched it die,
thumped its heart to work again.
Its life within her hand,
Jane felt a sudden rush
as she tossed it in the bin.

An overdose of morphine,
a carnal thrill to be in charge
of life and death, to lie beside them,
hug her victims closely as they died,
as if they were beloved.

She knew ecstasies beyond your grasp,
all hers alone, such satisfaction —
sending them down to near death,
bringing them back and letting them go.

Her goal to kill more people
than any mortal ever had;
though she ended many lives,
she failed her grand endeavor.

Tiny frog or suffering human,
Jane loved being God.

-Marge Simon

Helene Jagado 1803-1852

The Joys of Arsenic

Household servant, murderess, thief
a woman of ungodly deeds,
without purpose, without reason.

Employers, relatives and friends
fell victims to your toxin.
Sooner or later they took to bed
never to rise again.

you fed little Mary poisoned broth,
she barely five years old.
All innocence and piety,
You watched her writhe in agony
then joined the family weeping at her grave.

A hypocrite until the last,
no blessings on your grave —
in court you claimed you didn't even
know what arsenic was.

-Marge Simon

Amelia Dyer, Baby Farmer (1837 – 1896)

"I used to like to watch them with the tape around their neck."

At first, she took in "fallen" girls
until their little ones were born.
But then, why bother with the mothers?

Today she'd use *Craig's List*,
but then, the *Bristol Times & Mirror* ran Dyer's ads:
"Myself and my husband are dearly fond of children."
She said the couple lived across from an farm
so pretty when the cherry orchard bloomed.
The "couple" was Amelia, by herself, Amelia Dyer,
who feigned maternal sweetness,
her face lit with dreaming of the fee she'd get
from the unlucky mother.

The *farm* was baby farming.
And when mother came to get her child
the child was strangely missing, or a baby not her own.

The doctors almost found her out,
so many death certificates to sign,
so she took to stuffing little corpses into carpet bags
and throwing them into the River Thames.

And that was her mistake. For one such child was found
too late to save it. But police work
found evidence that led to Dyer's home and Dyer's hand.

You knew Amelia's work:
early days, she silenced them with Godfrey's Cordial, "Mother's
Friend."

But then, when opium worked too slow,
she wrapped white sewing tape around their tiny necks
and tightened it to still their mewling plaints.

"I used to like to watch them with the tape around their neck."

Was it three hundred? Four hundred? that Amelia sent to God?
She pled insanity
but died by strangulation like her "angels,"
ministered by James Billington's rope at Newgate.

Some later wondered, though:
our current science finds
a stamp licked by Jack the Ripper
bears female DNA.
Maybe women who in desperate condition
wished to end their pregnancies
might seek a Whitechapel surgery

and maybe those mutilated women,
their wombs dissected in obscenities we only whisper,
were not "Jack" the Ripper's work,
but Amelia. Amelia, who sent infants to heaven,
and perhaps a dozen luckless pregnant women, too.
Perhaps Amelia Dyer was the real Jack.

She liked to watch them with the tape around their neck.

-Mary Turzillo

Delfina and Maria Gonzalez - (circa 1960's)

A Rancho El Angel

We sisters ran a simple concern,
without bias to race or faith.
Those in health with a pleasing face
were the girls who got the job.

The lucky ones so procured
were force fed the heroin.
Those who got sick or lost their looks
soon met with termination.

As for the girls who got knocked up
we took care of the matter ourselves;
unscrupulous men and unborn babes,
our property home of their graves.

In prison, the cancer took me first, but
my sister went quietly mad,
due to the taunts of citizens
and wails of our spectral victims.

Addendum:

Delfina Gonzalez Valenzuela, the oldest 'Poquianchi' went mad, fearing she would be murdered in jail. On October 17, 1968, while she screamed and ranted, workers doing reparations above her cell in Irapuato jail, looked down to catch a glimpse of the notorious woman and accidentally dropped a bucket of cement on her head, killing her.

-Marge Simon

Tillie Klimek (1876 – 1936) and Nellie Koulik (dates unknown)

Trick or Treat

Tillie never claimed to be a psychic,
though she did prognosticate that nuisance pup would die
onTuesday, and he yap-yap-yapped his last,
right on the money.

Turned out she knew another magic trick.
Always claimed to make great candies.
With her cousin Nellie Koulik from the old country
she cooked some sweets, adding, sleight-of-handy,
a tincture to make one deathly sick.

Tillie hosted many a sumptuous dinner.
The term "groaning board" took on new meaning:
the groans came next morning,
as the guests moaned, some to die, some just to suffer.

Bluebeard was a man, but these cousins
were called the Bluebeard Murderers.
Why? Maybe they forgot to pluck their chin-hairs.
Instead of many wives, they buried lots of husbands
most met by lonely hearts ads in the papers.

Old Joseph Klimek, Tillie's fourth,
said her soup and coffee did taste queer.
He didn't put one and one together
until his insides just about caught fire.
They pumped his stomach
and found more there than chips and beer.
Plus, Tillie had bought insurance on the dear,
and already, pre his demise, procured a thirty dollar coffin.
She loved bargains.

When they came to take Tillie to the station
she told arresting officer Malone,
"I'll cook you up a bite to eat."

Tillie Klimek, Nellie Koulik:
their dishes seasoned well,
although with scant originality, by arsenic.

Tillie was the first female to hang in Illinois.
The hangman may have let her strangle slowly,
for after all, had she not, with all her magic tricks
for this life, had sufficient joy?

-Mary Turzillo

Helen Golay (1931-present) and Olga Rutterschmidt (1933-present)

Jimmy's Angels

They call this the city of angels,
and I first spied my two angels in church
where they mingled with us homeless bastards
just as if we were their kin.
They took pity on me,
took me to Burger King,
offered me a chance at a new life,
even a place to live.
I thought they had invisible wings,
invisible halos.
But why shouldn't I find in that church
a route to heaven on earth?

They were beautiful heavenly creatures,
one with the bouffant red hair,
the other with muscular legs from long valley hikes.
Lovely seraphim, a treat for the eyes,
especially in a dim church basement
although I heard one man whisper,
"Get a load of them Spandex crones."

So I moved into the nice rooms
out of the rain, with hot meals provided.
I paid no mind to the rumors:
Helen and Olga had also been angels
to Paul Vados
who was found in an alley
dead as road-kill.
Then there was word of Ken McDavid
run down by a Mercury Sable.

But no — how could it be?
Not poison, like in that old chestnut, *Arsenic and Old Lace.*

Nothing to do with my archangels of LA.

Until they came to me with papers to sign.
I was supposed to be related somehow to Helen
or maybe Olga. They wanted to insure my life.
As a big blessing.

So I moved out of that free apartment.
And the cops arrested Olga and Helen.
Funny, now that I think of them,
sitting in the soup kitchen, watching all us men closely.
I wonder if they really sang hosannahs,
if they really dwelt at God's right hand,
if they really belonged in that church at all
or if they were circling their prey,
their enormous, invisible wings
not the wings of angels
but vultures.

-Mary Turzillo

SISTER DREAD AND DAUGHTER DEATH

After Lizzie Bordon (1810-1927)

Lizzie's New Toy

Afternoon sun sifts through the blinds forming long white bars on the living room carpet. Seated in her favorite rocker, Lizzie picks Molly Dolly from the basket at her feet and combs its hair. The comb came with Molly and is pink, like all of the wonderful Molly Doll things are.

For her thirty-second birthday, Daddy and Mrs. Borden gave her the Magic White Horse with the beautiful mane and a real saddle that she could put on and take off. But Molly Dolly was too big and fat for the little white horse. Big and fat like Lizzie herself. This was not right, not like Molly Dolly's horse was supposed to be. Still, it is a very pretty horsie. It is not Molly Dolly's fault she is fat. It's Mrs. Borden and Daddy's fault for picking the horsie out. They must be punished.

Moonlight shines through the curtains on the blood soaked carpet, forming sparkles as pretty as Molly Dolly's blue eyes.

Addendum: Lizzie Borden was suspected of the axe killing of her father and step-mother, who she called "Mrs. Borden" on August 4th, 1892. She would have been thirty two that year. This prose poem is not based on true events.

-Marge Simon

Mary Bell (1957-)

"What's done to children, they will do to society."
– Karl A. Menninger

Mary's Tale

You didn't know my mom.
She was a whore, didn't want me,
made me do things with men,
when I was only four,
I just did what I was told.
So when I got older,
I had some things to do for myself.

My first was Martin Brown.
I was ten, he no more than four,
so pathetic, all alone,
nobody watching him in that dirty house,
condom wrappers on the floor,
broken glass and rats.
Maybe I saved him from a sad life.
But I didn't give a damn, back then.

I told my friend Norma,
She said she thought it would be fun
to kill another little boy,
carve our initials in his tummy,
make a mess of his little prick.
We took our time on Brian Howe,
I wrapped my fingers around his neck
until he stopped screaming.
It was what I wanted to do.
Nobody cared about me,
so why should this thing matter?

After twelve years in a place
with serene green walls and
starched blue uniforms,
cloistered, counseled,
I came of age and was released,
still wondering what it might be like
to be a normal little girl.

-Marge Simon

Christine Papin 1905-1937 Lea Papin 1911-1982

Sister, Mine

The bedroom door is open
I hear Madame and her daughter
yelling at Sister for no reason.
Christine calls my name, she needs me,
so I rush up the stairs.

I hold them down
as she gouges out their eyes.
I place Madame's in the folds
of her lovely paisley scarf.
So much noise they make,
it hurts my head,
and I begin to sob.

Sister quickly stills their cries.
We use the sharpest kitchen knife,
a hammer and the pewter pot
I polished earlier that day.

When we're done
she kisses me and takes my hand,
"Let's lie awhile and rest,
before M. Lancelin returns."
So tenderly she touches me,
removes my bloodied smock,
the dress and undergarments follow.

We lie as one, in spirit and in mind
until they find us, as they must,
sweet sister, my true love.

-Marge Simon

Regan, daughter of Leir (c. 700 BC)

Three Sisters, a Kingdom, and a Glass of Wine

Lear: Let them anatomize Regan. See what breeds about her heart. Is there any cause in nature that makes these hard hearts? (King Lear, III. iv)

I didn't hate Cordelia, really,
with her mush-mouthed *I love you only as is my bond*
and *why did my sisters marry, if they love their father all?*

After all, she got what she deserved,
which was

nothing
nothing
nothing

cause Daddy rejoined
nothing will come of nothing.

So sister Goneril and I divied up her share,
and maybe that will work,
though I never had much use for Goneril either.

Goneril and I got us good husbands, too,
ones with strong arms, bloody minds, and sharp teeth.
And Cordelia gets the King of France
who must be horny as a goat, because
he "loves her for herself alone,"
meaning
her curdled-milk cheeks and jewel eyes
meaning
and her hot and fertile snatch.

But now Cordelia (that pudding-faced bitch)
and France (that cunt-struck blood-hound) come back with an army
to take what's ours. Excuse me, I mean what's mine.

Because, let's face it, Goneril and I never did get along.

But, regardless, after all the confusion,
Edmund sends my henchman,
one of the disposable ones,
to hang Cordelia in her cell.

That will put quietus
to any claims she might advance,
even if she gets loose again.

Goneril was wrong about her husband Albany.
He's a fickle fool, loyal to Lear, not us.
I'm the widow; Cornwall was lusty, a-bed and in the field,
but died of a traitor servant's thrust.
So, nobles, what if you catch me naked
with this spunky half-noble, Edmund?
Goneril loves him too, but he's mine.

All this roil and bloodshed makes me thirsty.
That goblet—snatch it from bitch Goneril's claw.

-Mary Turzillo

Ching-Shih (1775–1844)

The Sister

They call her a fearless commander,
ut in those she leads, she inspires only terror.

They call her Madame Ching, Ching's widow,
ut she remembers how she escaped from the brothel.

hey say her beauty captured the pirate Ching
ut the last thing her victims see is the face of a devil.

hey say she seduced Ching to give her half his power
nd she used that power to kill thousands.

They say she commands respect.
Why would she not, when she nails men's feet to the deck?

When she then beats them to death?
When she beheads those who dishonor her law?

My sister was booty to one of Ching-Shih's men.
But another raped her, so he was beheaded.

This was not to defend my sister's honor.
No: Ching-Shih has laws for women who stray.

She ordered cannon-balls fastened to my sister's ankles.
then ordered her thrown into the sea.

Thousands revere Ching-Shih. Thousands follow her law.
She defeated the navy of the Middle Kingdom itself.

But she is a murderer. Her lover and her son

are consort and spawn of murderers.

I am alone now, outside my village, hiding in a rice paddy,
my husband, three sons, parents, in-laws, all slain by Ching-
Shih's pirates.

And my belly swells. One of her minions took me by force.
If Ching-shih learned this, that pirate would die. And myself —

So I hide, I live on gleanings and roots.
I will turn prostitute, for look how well that served Ching-Shih!

And the baby who grows in my belly? I will train him up
to defy Ching-Shih, fight his way to her chamber, and slay.

-Mary Turzillo

Jeanette McAdams (1833 — ?)

Jeanette in Trousers, Howling

We argued some over the bloomers, Mother Becky and me,
We McAdams be too frugal for such frippery, she said.
They would go out next fall, sure as little worms eat apples,
with her girls wearing mannish britches, and where?
Not to the church, she opined.

So I half-agreed, and set to sewing.
'Twould take most of a year to make clothes
for all three girls, plus Walter and young Arthur.
Mother Becky was a modest lady, and Father Alex,
well, he liked church suits but mostly needed working clothes.

They chambered me with young Jeannette.
Pretty thing,
but her eyes cold as ice on Lake Erie down the road.

So I lay one night trying not to wake young miss
and her sly as a rat gets up in the night
unlocks her chest and puts on trousers and a bowler.
Goes out the door, secret-like, for all the world
a man in her appearance and her stance.

I said nothing then.

But later I heard of the dying. Julia took ill with cramps
and Doc Coleman couldn't save the dear.
A beast howled outside her window, a wolf to call her home to God.
Though God was not the One who called, now I consider.

A tramp came to the funeral, dressed in bowler and dirty trousers
a tramp who had Jeanette McAdams' eyes.

I wish I'd said something then. Wish I'd told them
about Jeanette sneaking out all dressed up as a man.
But how could I know the relation?
I thought she'd gone to see her fella,
maybe some boy her father didn't like.

Or more like, she stole her father's cash
to buy strange finery.
But why did she poison not just her kin, but even the livestock?
Why did she hate her own father?
Ask the girl. Ask the devil.

Next Abigail tattle-taled on Jeanette
told of the chest with men's clothes locked inside.
Mother Becky looked, and lo, 'twas true,
trousers and a bowler.
So late that night, poor Abigail took poorly, then she died.

But no suspicion landed on Jeanette.
There was much sickness that fall. Who suspected?

And yet the other four children, and Mother Becky too,
each in turn fell ill when the tramp visited
and each time the wolf howled
and each time, where was Jeanette?
Gone visiting. Mysterious absence.
Six white stones in Edgewood Cemetery.

Bold as a sparrow, Jeanette wrote a letter
and Father McAdams opened it by chance,
It details all her plans to kill him too —
to inherit? who can know? I only tell the tale,
years too late to save a one of them.

He threw the bosom-viper out.

Years later, a dirty tramp came to his door.
His new wife, innocent of all, set the tramp to table
with a cup of milk and bread buttered and sugared.
But Father McAdams came home,
grabbed the beggar by nape and belt,
and threw the tramp like a hay-bale out his door.
He would not be Jeanette's last victim.

She never did wear those bloomers I proposed to make.
Mother Becky was right: they didn't suit the later age.
Fashions change.
But Jeannette did don pants made for a man,
and howled death, more like a beast than any man.

True, she did not kill her father.
She had reserved him for the last, the Lord knows why.

I tell this tale, listening for distant howling,
wondering at the new fashion of women wearing pants.
And I am less giving, Lord knows why,
when tramps come to my door.

-Mary Turzillo

THE LAST WIFE'S CLUB

Marie-Josephte Corriveau 1733-1763

"M" is for Murderess

Dear Marie- J, poor soul!
When Husband Number One passed on,
he was put to rest without ado,
and not a single villager knew why,

She took blame for killing husband Number Two –
found fatally flattened in the barn.
Though her dad did willingly assist,
he professed it wasn't his idea.

It was just a simple thing,
no demons summoned for the beating,
could have been a horse's kicks
that did such damage to the skull.
But such a surmise didn't hold.

In time, foul gossip spread; she was tried
and branded with the murderesses' "M".
That didn't seem enough, so she was hanged
and shackled in a strange iron coffin
most suitably contrived.

Marie-J earned a legend all her own,
her cage on display at Boston Museum,
"Macabre object from Quebec."

-Marge Simon

Delilah (dates unknown), source: Judges 13-16

The Hero's Head

So, his head in her lap
she thought of it sort of like a chicken
that had to be plucked.
All that unnecessary hair.

It wasn't the bribe, no.
Although that was kind of nice.

What was he, this husband?
Some sort of hippy
unwashed savage.
Claimed his strength was in the goddamn greasy locks.

And after he's been shaved nice and bald
(if he'd really cared,
he wouldn't have drunk all that wine
and fallen asleep so trusting-like)
she realized the head
should be gutted, too.

Of those eye-giblets.

-Mary Turzillo

Julia Agrippina (15-59 AD)

Agrippina Chats with a Portrait of the Former Empress

Messalina, dear, you got your just desserts,
sneaking off at night from your Imperial bed
to wear a she-wolf's name, and bed all comers
in an upscale house of prostitution.

Your boast? You bedded twenty-five one night.
How many knew you were the Emperor's wife,
when you spread your thighs in the house of Priapus?
And now you're dead and now I'm Rome's first lady.

Didn't Claudius smell the truth?
Well, maybe. He never cried when you were executed.
Plus, he married me. And disinherited Brittanicus
who you claimed is his son. You minx!

He likes my son much better, thanks a lot.
Nero will make a fine Emperor — so like a god!
Now let me see: I've gotten rid of you
without staining my white hands.

They claim I poisoned Passienus, my dear ex,
and killed Lollia, my rival for the hand of Claudius.
But Lucius? Please! That was suicide.
And it was only right Sosibius should die:

Sosibius was poisoning Brittanicus' mind,
teaching he could supplant my own dear son,
my precious Nero, for the crown.
Then there was that slight dispute about those gardens.

Did Taurus kill himself because of me?
Oh dear! I only hinted — but that was just enough.
Now, where's my ornatrix? It's time to dress my hair
to make me chic for Claudius' dinner party.

What shall we have tonight? I ordered honeyed wine,
lobster, wild pig, and dormice rolled in poppyseeds.
And don't forget those mushrooms, plump and earthy,
I gathered just this morning. Ah, too rich for me!

But Claudius will find I picked them just for him.

-Mary Turzillo

Gesche Margarethe Gottfried, born Gesche Margarethe Timm (1785-1831)

Gesche's Deathmask

Behold the death-mask of Gesche Gottfried,
Long lost, returned to us from England's grim phrenologists.
Look at the gentle soft smile, you honored visitors,
the kindly gaze.

She was beset by sorrows,
shadowed by clouds of misery.
Her surname signifies God's peace
and she did carry peace to those most dear to her
nursing those who suffered grave disease.

Her husband was beset by wrenching cramps;
she nursed him day and night, in faithful sorrow, until
he gave up breath. She bore her widowhood with bowed head,
then grieved the deaths of brother, father, son, and daughters,

and married Micheal Christoph.
But he, alas, was taken ill; his spirit fled.
Sweet lady had a brave and hope-filled heart,
so was betrothed again, but that good bachelor likewise died.

How could she bear these sorrows?
Her friends in Bremen called her an angel
for her constant care to those she was to lose.
Fate had cursed this gentle-minded soul.

Alas, her friends languished as her family had!
Her music teacher, maid, and landlady were taken.
She was a soul beset with cares unparalleled.

At last, the kindly Friedrich Kleine loaned her cash to live.
But he, alas, succumbed to the pain of twisted bowels.
And who knows? Her debt to him must be forgiven.

A doctor, though, questioned the butter she mixed
in victuals of the invalids she nursed.
Mouse-butter, it was called. Quite tasty,
although the fat was flecked with specks of arsenic.

Yes, they called her Angel of Breman,
for she did bring God's peace to many a soul.
And now her severed head is lost, but never mind.

Here you see captured in cold plaster
the sweetness of this angel's loving face,
perhaps in contemplation of the fifteen she sent before,
those she dispatched to heaven's grim-eyed grace.

-Mary Turzillo

Sada Abe, 1905-1970 or later.

Mad Love

See, look in my purse.
I carry him everywhere,
death alone will part us.

He would not leave his wife
I could not live while he touched her
or others, because his sex was so perfect.

It tasted like the sea,
and when I look back, I felt myself a dolphin
fighting the line,
landed after a long struggle, by his strength.

No other man satisfied me.
But he would not promise
to be mine alone, forsaking the others.

I bought an expensive sushi knife—
I put it to his throat.
He thought I was kidding.

We spent those last nights
playing deadly games.
I cut off his blood supply with my obi cord.

He said it made coming more heavenly
and so did I, so did I.
But I went too far. Did I mean to? Was it murder?

I kiss it, I tongue it, I put it to my cleft
but it's no good, the limp thing

is no good when he's gone.
Perhaps a museum will display it.

Most prized, most loved part
all wilted now.
I wrote my name in his blood,
though not much blood now he's dead.

Yet, it wasn't like sushi; sushi doesn't bleed.

Am I evil?
Please don't judge
until you loved as I have loved.
Nothing like hatred,
just madness. Mad love.

-Mary Turzillo

Katherine Knight 1955-

Katherine Knight's Demon

Her childhood rapes,
so many sleepless nights.
In that terrible dark after,
I entered her mind.

She had such a pretty smile when she was being good,
working in an abattoir, found a lifelong love of knives;
with such a pretty smile, she sliced and diced the flesh,
slept with her tools "in case of need".

Get it out of your system, I whisper

She left her baby on a railroad track
because its crying hurt her head,
but it survived and was returned.

Get on with it!

A string of husbands, lovers,
each of them scarred by her blades,
yet not a one dared turn her in.

Get it over!

John was the last to turn away,
yet she begged him to return,
and he could not resist her charms,
that pretty smile, when she was good.

She stabbed him over and over again,
removed his skin and hung it up to dry,

cleaved off his head and cooked it in a pot
with carrots, onions, thyme
to feed his children, none her own.

Afterwards, she took the pills and slept,
a tower of former lovers in her dreams,
their bloodless bodies pale as bone.

How she loved the summer nights
the taste of salt and sweat,
the bloody tears of weeping flesh —

Out of her system, just like that.

-Marge Simon

Vera Renczi (c1903-c1930)

Zinc caskets in the basement.

Vera, dear Vera, what are you thinking of?
Why do you question your own husband's love?

Karl, my dear husband, I know you're untrue:
be that as it may, have some wine with your stew.

What happened to Karl, good Vera, my friend?
I learned in a car wreck my Karl met his end.

Vera, my Vera, what sorrow on your house
but I could make up for it as your new spouse

New husband, I know your affections have turned.
But have a nice tipple; it's just what you've earned.

Vera, dear Vera, all these men at your door.
Yes, neighbor, but not one man is true in a score.

Mother, dear mother, tell me of my descent.
Who was my father, reveal where he went.

Lorenzo, my darling, your father was killed:
in a tragic collision his heart blood was spilled.

Mother, dear mother, what is that faint stink?
And lo, tell me why all these caskets of zinc?

Though your innocent mind knows no evil or such,
Lorenzo, my darling, you've seen far too much.

So since you've enjoyed my vintage libation

I must bid you farewell despite deep tribulation.

But let me hold you once last loving time
ere you go to your rest in a casket, zinc-lined.

What can be said of Vera Renczi's obsessions?
In her basement they found 32 zinc-lined coffins.

-Mary Turzillo

Nasra Yussef Mohammed Al-Enezi (1986-2010)

How to Bake a Wedding Cake

Implements needed:

1 polygamous society
1 23-year old pregnant, jealous wife
1 new bride
1 adoring husband (adores both wife and bride)
1 large tent, one exit only, not up to fire-code standards

Ingredients:
1 tender but obdurant heart (marinate in jealousy)
5 gallons petrol
(alternative carb-free recipe) 5 gallons of cursed water
tears of rage to taste

Procedure: Wait until all guests (women and children only) are seated. Pour petrol around four sides of tent.
Broil at 900° F for three minutes.
Allow bride to escape, seared.

Serves 60-90, including small children.

(From Satan N Satin, *Hearts on Fire: a Cookbook of Carnage*, 2010)

-Mary Turzillo

Bonnie Elizabeth Parker, (1910 – 1934)

The Marriage of Suicide Sal

Clyde's heart was gutted by the prison rape,
his vindication the death he dealt his rapist,
an act repeated with each man he killed.
He gave you bank notes instead of flowers.
Murder was your engagement ring,
a bank the wedding chapel, and robbery your nuptial bond.
Hard-scrabble exile was your honeymoon.
You renewed your vows with every killing he committed,
your children were those deaths instead of births:
you, accomplice, though you never pulled the trigger.
He brought you atropine and bandages instead of champagne.
Your love-nest was The Red Crown Tavern,
and the stolen Ford V8 was both your marriage bed and bier.
Did he love you?
Can a rattlesnake know love?
You thought he loved you.

You, like a thousand other gun-struck babes,
adored a killer better than the boredom of living as a waitress.
You were addicted to his bad-boy magic.
The danger of his kisses made your panties wet.
You thrilled with every headline.
You mocked the courage
of every cop who swore he'd take him down.
You penned poetry to show your soul's devotion.
You danced to echoed music
of the drumbeat of Clyde's Browning,
thrilled to the howling violence of his face in front page photos.
You writhed beneath him, blind with bloody passion,

his murders sweet like drugs,
climaxing in the gun-fire on Route 154,
your orgasm the blast of bullets to your heart.
You thought you loved him.

-Mary Turzillo

Velma West (1927-1959)

Queen of Clubs

Thirteen cards dealt to each. Bridge: a game for modern women.
"How's the hubby?" asks Velma's friend Miss W.
"Eddie's a bit down," says Velma. And she bids, "One club."

"I pass," says the lady to the left.
"Two hearts," says Mabel Young,
her gaze lingering on Velma's face.
"Three diamonds," says Miss E.

"Four clubs," says Velma, and her gaze is molten on Mabel.
(This eye contact: some illegal signal?
No, among such ladies, who would dare cheat
or do some dire deed?)
"Four no trump," says Miss W.

"Pass," says Mabel.
"Six clubs," says Velma. And three passes.
A slam. And play begins.

Miss W. throws down the ten of spades,
but Velma takes the trick with the queen of spades
drawn from the dummy.

The play goes on, until three hearts lay on the table,
Velma takes the trick with the ace of clubs.

"Won't you stay the night?" asks Mabel.
Of course. That was the plan all along.
Eddie won't need the Hupmobile in the morning, will he?

But next morning, Eddie's boss sends James around

to know why Eddie didn't come to work.
And look here: Eddie's head wrapped in a gory pillowcase,
a claw-hammer and a table-leg smeared with Eddie's blood.

Eddie was no King of Hearts. No, more like the deuce.
Or, let's say, the Joker, because that's one card
left out of any bridge deck.

-Mary Turzillo

Winnie Ruth Judd (1905-1998)

Winnie and the Big Black Trunk

The cops said it was like this:
Winnie and Agnes got into it over Happy Jack.
Winnie was married to a sawbones named Billy,
but who the hell cares?
Happy Jack, he was so much fun
both in the sack and out.

So anyway, they got into it
over Jack of the Italian suits and long dick
and push came to shove and Winnie, just playing around,
acting like she was really mad,
shot Agnes seven times. Oh shit.

About that time, who should come home
but Hedvig,
Hedvig the third roommate.
Winnie turned to her all desperate:
"Agnes stole my man, and anyway it was an accident.
Heddy, you gotta help me."
So they cut up the body
cause otherwise it wouldn't fit
into that black trunk,
and then Heddy said,
"You said it was an accident, but I count seven bullet holes."

"Let's have a drink," said Winnie.
And then they got into it about Happy Jack,
because Heddy liked him too,
and one thing led to another
and rat-a-tat-tat, Heddy was face down in the bathtub.

Well, if you don't like that story,
try this:
Maybe Agnes and Happy Jack were having a drink,

all alone in the house,
or maybe a little tumble in the hay,
when along comes Heddy and says to Jack,
"You louse! You said you loved me!"
and then maybe it's Heddy that takes up the .25
but Happy Jack gets the gat away from her
and rat-a-tat-tat he shoots Heddy right in the left tit —
and then Winnie comes home —

No, wait. What about Winnie's hubby,
that cool hand sawbones, Billy?
Maybe he came home, saw what his squeeze had done
and helped her cover it up
using his expert sawbones skills
by slicing up the ladies and jamming them into that black trunk.

Well, does it matter?
Two dead babes, one big black trunk.
Winnie was on the run.
She got caught when the conductor asked,
What's that smell, coming from your luggage, Miss?

Police, judge, jury, they all thought the same.
Winnie got the death sentence.

But then she got off. Mercy, mercy, Mister Jury-man!
They put her in the nuthouse
from which she ran off at least six times.

And must have had a fine old time.
Lived to be 93.
What kind of a life is that?
Pretty good, I'd say, for a woman with a history.

But what I'm wondering is,
Who got Happy Jack?

-Mary Turzillo

Jodi Arias (July 9, 1980-present)

June Wedding, far from the Temple

The thousand miles you drove became a wedding march,
the hiss of tires on pavement, Lohengrin.
You were too furious-eager for the hesitation step
but rushed to your refusing bridegroom's bed
to consummate before the knot was tied.

This was the order of your ceremony:
the wedding photographs were sex-hot selfies,
your wedding gown the Emperor's clothes,
the chapel was the bedroom floor:
no clergy need seal the rite.
Each dagger thrust, an act of love
or rape. Each scream a serenade,
each gaping wound an open mouth to kiss,
the gun-shot to the head the wedding temple bell,
the spray of his heart's blood the rain of rice,
the shower floor the honeymoon motel.

You think have your wish: celestial marriage.
You and your Alexander joined for all eternity
to mate and rape and sodomize and breed,
your spiritual family a parody of Mormon love.
For only demons could be thence conceived,
whether in hate, or madness, or Narcissus' rage.

We hope another woman will come forth
and marry Alexander posthumously, as writ allows,
to save him from your psychopathic vows.

-Mary Turzillo

DAMES FROM THE DEEPEST CIRCLE OF HELL

Delphine Lalaurie   c. 1775 – c. 1842

Delphine Lalaurie's Upstairs Room

Her slaves they were,
with spiked collars
to remind them who was boss,
nails pulled out by the roots
two boys with mutilated privates
none knew their names –

but there was pretty Kitta,
strung out on a bed,
intestines wrapped around her waist,
her brother, Sol, with
empty holes where once
his brown eyes shone,
guts nailed to the floor,
and her mother, partly skinned,
and amputated arms
"like a human caterpillar"
someone later notes,

and young Sam,
hair already white,
chained like the rest
to the wall,
lips sewn shut
over a mouthful of dung.

No voices left to speak
the horrors of that room.
Is all false or is some true?
only the ghosts of the victims know,
if only their bones could tell.

-Marge Simon

Ilse Koch 1906-1967

Red Witch of Buchenwald

Pure Aryan, a redhead
and wife of a Commandant,
she toured the camp at Buchenwald
with swinging hips and teasing smile,
but should one man stare,
should one Jew-boy dare –
he was a dead man, then and there
or shortly after.

And they all knew it.

She selected certain ones,
but only those with tattoos —
for she wanted the skins.
Such unique lampshades
from the factory at Buchenwald,
leather goods of human hides
for the Reich's officious wives!

And they all knew it.

The townsfolk were invited
to view the rich display.
They marched to see with happy smiles,
Then shocked and hushed,
they hustled away home.

-Marge Simon

Elizabeth Bathory 1560-1614

Lady Bathory's Procurer

Have a seat here, my lovely,
beside this precious little stream.
My wife? No, she never comes
here, I promise you that.

I've brought a flask drawn
from a keg of our finest wine,
sweet as our stolen kisses,
I'm sure you'll agree.

My wife would adore you.
No, that's untrue — I cannot lie to
this face, the bold red lips, the
thick lashes hiding such feelings.
You are liking this drink, yes?
There's another in my sack.

It is a special sack that my wife
designed to take on my walks.
Note how delicate the tiny stitches,
rose petals pale as milk.

Ah, I see you're asleep,
you'll neither wake nor weep
once your life blood's drained,
rest assured the honor is yours
you'll have given your life
to preserve the looks
of my youthful, beautiful wife.

-Marge Simon

Myra Hindley 1942-2002

"The Most Evil Woman in Britain"

What a babe!
"Delightful personality,"
said Lord Longford,
who campaigned to set her free,
absolution for her sins.

Such a tease, that British gal,
a 60's bubbly bottle blonde;
for her thrills, the perfect crimes,
three neighbors' children victims
in forever bedtime graves.

Oh yes, she made the best
of prisons, once found out.
With lovers of both sexes,
Guards or cellmates,
sweet forbearance.

Dead now, she's free —
a simple confession,
all her sins forgiven.
In Myra's perfect Heaven,
she dupes angelic suckers
with her sparkling persona.

-Marge Simon

Wu Zetian, woman Emperor, (624-705).

Dragon in Phoenix Skin

Hands soft as silk,
heart hard as jade —
you brought the Middle Kingdom glory,
your hand enemy to corruption,
friend to schools and the arts.
But how many did you murder
on your road to the throne?

Smooth as a seed-pearl,
sharp as iron plowshares,
your rule sprouted from flattery
then bore fruit from rats' tattle.
You planted copper boxes
for denouncing your enemies,
whether guilty or not.
Thus hundreds were slain:
beheaded, or told they must end their own lives,
their children transformed into slaves.

Face of a flower,
heart of an ice storm.
Ministers, concubines, rivals, or courtiers,
husband, sister, son-Emperor, all:
your enemies wither and drop
like winter crystanthemums.

Touch sweet as peach-flesh,
soul of a spider,
did you not flinch
when your newborn daughter
gazed up at you

as your hands held the strangling sash
so you could frame your rival concubine?

Eye of the phoenix,
heart of a dragon:
when you commissioned the Enlightened One's statue,
emblem of your dynasty's splendor,
and ordered his face a portrait of yours,
did the Buddha forgive you?

-Mary Turzillo

Lady, Wife to MacBeth (birth and death circa 1000)

Lady M

When I was but new, a wee slip of a thing,
we played lords and ladies, queens and kings.
I begged to be king but my brother said No.
Girls can't be kings. Go wash your tear-streaked face.

So I bided my time and thought: my brother is wrong.

When I grew to have breasts and hips, my father said lo:
you will marry this lord and live in a northern manse.
Do not cry, for this man is a noble warrior lord.
Go, wash your face, that you look comely for him.

But the castle was cold summer, fall, and spring,
and the darkened woods crept like swords marching near,
and witches wailed and cackled outside at night,

and they took my babes away to wetnurse,
while I bent to the running of my warrior lord's manse.

I thought, if I cannot be king perhaps I'll be queen
and I whispered and kissed and scolded and nagged
and beseeched and shamed my noble lord,

and now, downstairs, he whets knives against stone.

We will have ghosts at table, phantom daggers before his eyes.
He will be king, and I will be queen
and I'll wash and wash till my hands be clean.

-Mary Turzillo

Cathy Wood and Gwendolyn Graham – call & response Simon & Turzillo

Cathy Wood 1962 –

Five days of Forever Love

Under your spell, to prove my devotion,
I distracted the supervisors while you worked,
smothering or strangling those in useless lives,
poor frail dears with failing minds and memories.

We had our secrets then,
our love bond: five victims, one a day –
as they lay in Alpine Manor's beds.

You called me baby names,
honey toes and sweetie bee —
your lips found my secret places,
I floated on your voice,
did everything you asked.

But you took another woman in my place –
that bitch who implicated me as well
and that I can't forgive.

-Marge Simon

Gwendolyn Graham, 1963-

Breathless

You took my breath away.
My heart almost stopped
You smothered me with sweet loving:
Ooooh so intense:
make me come while I smother—
make it better!

We took their breath away
those old hags
poor girls, they weren't getting nooky,
so why not relieve them
let them out of this world
take their sad old twisted bodies
away.

Then we slipped into an empty room
maybe a room another old gal had just died in
and I'd put my hands here and here and here
in the secret places that made you quiver
that made you convulse
while I smothered you.

I did Margarite, the first
and Edith, and Myrtle, and Belle, how many others.
took trophies: jewelry,
a miniature of grandkids in a cheap pendant,
a hearing aid, some dentures.

Then I got thinking, darling,
so I said, Cathy,
Cathy, you do the next one.

And suddenly it was NO

and I realized
what a fat ugly bitch you had always been,
that our secret was too much
for your cowardly cunt head.

And I found a better lover.

And now you tell these lies.

Yes, they were lies.
All those women died naturally,
we just fantasized
head trips
to make our sex-seizures more red-hot.

They were just sick jokes.
You tried to make them real.
You said
I was the one with the smothering washcloth
I was the dominant.
But you were the boss
don't deny it.

You were the fat ugly bitch,
lonely,
who fastened on me
like a vaginal leech
and now your "confession"
teased out of you by the dicks in blue
has ruined me forever.

May you die gasping for breath
and not with your thighs spread
not with my tongue on your nipple

not with my own hands
crushing your blubbering lips and nose

but just struggling to live
like those pitiful crones,
losing everything, even their pitiful dentures,
losing even grandkids in lockets.

Breathless. Truly and evermore breathless.

-Mary Turzillo

Cathy Wood: Still Breathing

You talk about it all crazy,
keep saying things like
how I made that all up,
like you don't remember.

Never mind those old hags,
all whiney and prune faced,
couldn't pee without our help,
they were like little kids,
didn't know where they came from
or where they were going
on any day or night.

They're all dead and gone,
we just helped them along
to their precious pearly gates,
a little sooner didn't hurt.

You being so strong, so smart,
you said we should choose them
by their initials, to spell "M.U.R.D E.R."
but it didn't work out right.

I'd never have done this,
but you enchanted my heart,
in your thrall, I wrote poetry —
"Love you forever and a day".

I know that and so do you.
We were a team, you and me,
and both of us are still alive.
I'll get out before you do.

See you in hell, bitch.

-Marge Simon

Mary Farmer Took An Axe

A Lizzie Borden fan?
she likely didn't even know of her,
being an immigrant and Irish,
lucky to live in a run-down shack,
Barton Tavern on Paddy's Hill.

Lead her to Doc Fell's contraption:
they must die who choose to kill.

She had an axe and used it well
on neighbor Sarah Brenton
whose husband had a love of ale,
so who's to blame poor Paddy
if he lost track of her?

Braid her locks and shave her temples
the chair is wood, the mask is rubber.

Paddy didn't have a clue
til Mary Farmer came to say
his wife was done with him,
had left for parts unknown, and
deeded all to her.

Apply electrodes to her brow
and strap her to the lightning chair.

The poor man was evicted.
his wife's remains within a trunk,
when Mary and her man moved in.
But when Paddy sobered up,
he brought the law.

The electrician pulls the switch,

the priest hears every breath she draws.

Mary, Mary, strange but true,
only woman in your county,
second woman in New York,
to end your life with Tesla's snakes
shooting death sparks through your cells.

Two thousand volts the man sends through her,
then sends again two jolts of juice
before her body stops convulsing
and her soul drops down to Hell.

-Marge Simon & Mary Turzillo

Aileen Wurmos (1956-2002)

"I killed those men, robbed them as cold as ice. And I'd do it again, too. There's no chance in keeping me alive or anything, because I'd kill again. I have hate crawling through my system...I am so sick of hearing this 'she's crazy' stuff. I've been evaluated so many times. I'm competent, sane, and I'm trying to tell the truth. I'm one who seriously hates human life and would kill again." – Aileen Wuornos

Born Mean

I was s bastard child,
born to a fourteen year old mother,
sired by a convicted felon;
I wasn't born crazy,
I was born mean.

Ladies you don't want to know
what your man is doing when he's on the road
you think he's working hard to keep you happy
get real —he's just another john.

I put one of them down, and seven more,
between my legs with bullets in their lungs,
their balls, their fucking brains
yes, yes, yes and I'd do it again.

Florida isn't all you think,
it runs hot and it runs cold,
I got to get the hate out
it steams under my skin.

Truck stop lot lizards
got nothing on me –

I taught some of them,
screwed the rest.

These nice Rest Areas,
friendly folks,
polite as white rice.
This state's all for free,
your trip's on me, boy.

You fucking Bible folk
preaching and praying forgiveness —
maybe you'll say you forgive,
and maybe you won't,
but you'll never forget me.

-Marge Simon

Bell Gunness (1859-1908) & Nannie Doss (1905-1965)

Kindred Spirits

Belle Gunness, the murderess,
stood taller than most men —
six feet high and sixteen stone,
a female beardless Bluebeard.

Made rich by her husband's passing,
she advertized far and wide,
her suitors were many, but all of them failed
to walk her down the aisle;
each disappeared, done in by her hand
as her family had gone before them.

Yet one man admired her,
though suspecting her ways —
expiry by arson or poison,
he loved her all the same.

Elusive in death,
Belle's bones now lie
in a place no flowers grow.

As if there was a need for such,
(Ma Belle was quite a woman)
along came little Nannie Doss,
three years old when "Hell's Belle" passed.
Surely her life echoed much the same
with marriages that failed.

Four husbands, two children,
her mother, her sisters, and more —
with insurance on love everlasting,

her rat poison never failed.

She claimed she loved them all,
like stories in romance magazines
but the Black Widow died in prison,
still searching for "Perfect Love".

-Marge Simon

Caril Ann Fugate 1943 —

Caril Fugate's Angel

So grown up at thirteen, Caril knows
her heart, knows how to use a knife
because her special angel taught her
jab to the navel,
twist and pull.

On the wrong road, under a bad moon,
she and Charlie hitch a ride.
Caril eyes their victims,
Charlie's shotgun trained on them,
a robbery of no account.

Bad mood raging, shots fired,
Charlie's done.
But Caril wants fun of her own,
the girl is still alive.

Takes her little dagger,
twists and pulls,
one more scream before the end,
or just a disappointing moan?

Only Caril's special angel knows.

-Marge Simon

Lavinia Fisher 1793 – 1820

A Legend in My Time

My John and I had quite a plan
that worked out well for years,
our Six Mile Tavern offered
dinner, tea and special lodgings.

Drugged by my tea, the victims slept,
then John would stab and rob them.
The local folks, they had no clue,
our private lives remained unknown.

There came a man who hated tea,
dumped his out when I was unaware.
I spoke with him for hours more,
still he bore his wits about him.

I finally put him up in a room
with the bed that splits in two,
sending its cargo down below
to a pit, with spikes for a carpet.

All would have played as fitting,
yet the traveler was still alert.
He chose a chair to sleep in,
awoke to see his bed collapse.

Well before the dawn, he'd fled,
reported all he'd been through,
I should have listened to husband John,
never misjudge a scholar.

"A married woman can't be hanged,

it's the letter of the law," I railed.
So to the hangman went my John
the day before our turn.

On the stage, my parting words:
"If you've a message for Lucifer,
let me know, for I'll see him soon!"
Then I jumped from the scaffold,
having had my final say.

-Marge Simon

Leonarda Cianciulli 1894-1970

Coveted Cianciulli Recipes

Crunchy Tea Cakes

Drug selected victim with wine. Chop off head with sharp axe. Continue chopping until pieces are small enough for three gallon pots. Add seven kilos caustic soda. Stir until pieces are dissolved. It should appear as a thick, dark mush. Pour into buckets and dispose of discretely.

As for the blood in the basin, let it coagulate. Dry in oven. Grind, mix with 3 cups flour, 2 cups sugar, 4 bars chocolate, 1 ½ cups milk and six eggs. Add one stick margarine. Mix well, knead together. Daub onto baking sheet and cook in 350 degree oven for twenty minutes. Yields approximately four dozen tea cakes. Serve them to the Church ladies who come to visit.

Creamy Perfumed Soaps

Select a mature woman with fat, white flesh. Drug victim. Use same modus operandi as with recipe for tea cakes. Add 1 large bottle of your favorite cologne. Simmer 40 minutes. Pour into muffin pans or molds of your choice. Cool. Makes 3 dozen bars or more, depending on size. Be sure to make teacakes from the blood, which will be really sweet. You may wish to cut down the amount of sugar.

The beautiful copper ladle that you use for scraping the fat off the kettles can be donated to the government, in case of a need for metal, should there be another war.

-Marge Simon

Griselda Blanco   1943-2012

Memories

Her father's eyes
on Monday morning
empty as the bottle
he finished off
the night before.

Her mother's hand
an instant before it tore
her cheek so hard
it became a scar
that never healed.

The tears of the child she held for ransom
and when that didn't work, she shot him dead.
He came from the rich, and she from a slum.
She was only eleven at the time,
but she remembers.

From pickpocket to prostitute,
she joined the '80's major leagues,
and so became Miami's queen of mean,
in the drug wars of the Cocaine Cowboys,
and that she also remembers.

Big hips, red lips and a winsome smile,
she played the game, called the shots
but who knows if she remembers
how she couldn't dodge those last
assassin's bullets to her head.

-Marge Simon

Melissa Huckaby 1987 –

Little Sandra Cantu

I don't know why I did it.
Really, I don't know.
I practiced on a neighbor girl,
to be certain it would work.
She drank my medicated water,
but I couldn't do it at the time,
it was after Sunday school,
no mystery there.

Once it was done and over with
I gave them lots of clues,
but not a single person listened
to what I said about her body,
the one I finally chose to kill.

I took her to the church,
for a Xanax communion.
There was a rolling pin involved,
something nasty happened
to her private parts before
the Angel of Death arrived.

I prayed as I arranged her
inside my Eddie Bauer leather bag
and left it in a nearby pond.

I don't know why.
I really don't.

-Marge Simon

Mary Tudor, "Bloody Mary" Queen of England and Ireland (1516-1558)

Remembering Lady Jane Grey, as We Lay Dying

We do regret those tiny souls, not noble,
that flew like burning cinders, not to heaven,
but floated down to sullied earth like rubble,
then unto netherworlds, alas, unshriven.

In five years reign did We save England's soul
from those who wrenched God's words in false translation:
those bodies broken, but The Faith still whole,
and Tyndall's heresies purged from Our nation.

Archbishop Cranmer maintained his base protest:
But Holy Ghost made Us this nation's ruler.
We could not at the last say he confessed.
Burning is cruel, but soul's damnation crueler.

Athwart Our dead-bloat womb, succession's line is broken.
Despite Our piety, perhaps Our God has spoken.

-Mary Turzillo

Phoolan Devi, (10 August 1963 – 25 July 2001)

Rebirth

You, bitch, in the chic purple sari of pure silk, your long hair shining with rose-scented oil, with all your gold bangles. You, with your ethnic pretensions, eating your restaurant thali, ignoring me, me, the soul lurking in your vindaloo. You fucking cunt, look, see me here, here in the sauce! I survived beatings and rape when I was a child, my spirit unchilled by upper caste tyrants like you, though I admit they were men, not a woman. Look down at your plate, toy at it with your impotent fork, and find me. I killed many men, but fucked more. I rounded up the relatives of my high-caste enemies and shot them dead. I made many widows that Valentine's Day. Later, I surrendered and went to prison. But the people freed me and I was elected to the Parliament. And then I died by an assassin's bullet. I thought I would merge with God, with Durgha, for they had called me the incarnation of the Goddess, She Who preserves and annihilates. Karma says we must work through many lives til we are perfect. I thought I would be subsumed into the essence of the goddess. Or if not, I would be a lioness such as Durgha rides. But instead I was for decades trapped in the body of a neem tree. And after I was cut down in that life, I was reborn as the poor wretched chili you see here in your sauce.

Only a red pod,
the fire on a Brahmin's tongue
how can I evolve?

-Mary Turzillo

Squeaky Fromme (October 22, 1948 - present)

Empty Pistol

When you went after Ford,
did you forget to load that Colt 45?
You said you didn't mean to hurt him
but how the hell else
were you going to get his attention?

And you weren't there when the Family
slaughtered Sharon and her unborn son
But you did uphold Manson's innocence
beneath the courtroom steps
by carving X in your fair brow.

And you weren't there
when James and Lauren Willett were killed and buried,
nor did you help to kidnap their baby.

Seems like babies were in your horoscope.

Sure, you have your wiki article
plus you're a character in a musical (*Assassins*),
which is more than most good people
get from saving Redwoods.

But here's the thing:
you can't improve the world with murder
or by consorting with the fiends who kill.

That unloaded weapon
just showed how impotent pistols really are:
they never make things better,
never change the President's mind,

never make babies into good adults.

They only make headlines
and buckets of blood
and make people shake their heads
at you, you clueless Valley Girl, failed hippy,
with helter-skelter brains.

-Mary Turzillo

Queen Ranavalona I (1778-1861)

The Choice

The rope cuts high across my chest,
the pain burns my shoulder joints.
I know why they have brought me here.

I swing, dizzy with terror, over the chasm.
I dare look down:
frigatebirds and stormy petrals,
an albatross, even a rare vanga,
wheel above the boulders,
scavenging remains of those who went before.
But I am dangling higher still,
between the rocks and heaven.

Must that be my fate,
to fall and burst like ripe passionfruit?

Twelve pagan hideous sampy,
led by Kelimalaza, the "little famous one,"
are Queen Ranavalona's gods.
My God is three in One,
my crucifix an emblem of His love.

"Choose!" says the executioner,
axe primed to cut the rope,
and send me to be crushed on rocks below.

Shall I bow before Ranavalona's sampy
and live a few more years,
crawling before her tyrant throne?
Or shall I die a martyr's death
and live forever in a higher kingdom?

"I choose my savior, Jesus Christ," I shout.
The rope around my torso jerks;
the axe has struck,
at first the freedom of the air,
then wind screams around my ears,
then shock and agony and then –

-Mary Turzillo

Unknown Victim/Perpetrator (dates unknown)

The Woman's Fault

Above all, it's the women's fault,
the American ones, who bare their faces,
their hair, even their arms and legs and the tops of their breasts.
They kill their children even before conception.
They instruct their husbands how to run the family.
Sometimes the husbands, stupidly, listen.

The Satan-possessed mothers do not cut out from their daughters
the obscene parts which make these women beasts.
They swagger and flaunt their lewd needs.

Because of these she-wolves, America has gotten greedy rich.
The bitches go out and get money just like men.
They teach their daughters to read and do math,
they assure them they can do whatever a man can.

But maybe that idea bears some truth
because an occasional pious girl among us
is inspired to do a jihadist's duty.

The western devils teach them women could go to heaven, like a
man,
that the same rewards await them there.
So, take this package, Fatima. Put it under your chador
and nobody will suspect you. You are short,
and even with the black cloth brushing your ankles,
your feet and unmanicured hands, naked of a slut's red polish,
look delicate and weak, all womanly.

You are our inspiration,
We only want to protect you,
the virtuous woman who knows your place,
in a thousand bloody gobbets, strewn over the plaza.

-Mary Turzillo

MARGE SIMON

Marge Simon lives in Ocala, Florida and is married to Bruce Boston. She edits a column for the HWA Newsletter, "Blood & Spades: Poets of the Dark Side," and serves as Chair of the Board of Trustees. She won the Strange Horizons Readers Choice Award, 2010, the SFPA's Dwarf Stars Award, 2012, and the Elgin Award for best poetry collection, 2015. She has won the Bram Stoker Award ® for Poetry, the Rhysling Award and the Grand Master Award from the SF Poetry Association, 2015. She has work in the anthology Scary Out There, a story and poems in YOU, HUMAN and fiction in Chiral Mad 4, 2017, Dark Regions Press www.margesimon.com

MARY TURZILLO

My 1999 Nebula-winner,"Mars Is no Place for Children" and my Analog novel, An Old-Fashioned Martian Girl, are read on the International Space Station. My poetry collection, Lovers & Killers, won the 2013 Elgin Award. I have been a finalist on the British Science Fiction Association, Pushcart, Stoker, Dwarf Stars, Nebula, and Rhysling ballots. Sweet Poison, my Dark Renaissance collaboration with Marge Simon, was a Stoker finalist and won the 2015 Elgin Award. I'm working on a novel, *A Mars Cat and his Boy.* My novel *Mars Girls,* will be coming out in 2017 from Apex. I live in Ohio, with my scientist-writer husband, Geoffrey Landis and in my spare time compete internationally as a foil fencer.

Printed in Great Britain
by Amazon

16615134R00068